P9-BYC-870

ZOOS
OF
THE WORLD

BY THE SAME AUTHOR
In the Wilds of Africa
In the Wilds of North America

ZOOS
OF
THE WORLD

by Robert Halmi

Four Winds Press ❀ New York

590.7
7

Library of Congress Cataloging in Publication Data

Halmi, Robert.
　Zoos of the world.

　SUMMARY: A history of zoos and a survey of zoos
throughout the world today.
　1. Zoological gardens—Juvenile literature.
[1. Zoological gardens] I. Title.
QL76.H34　　　590'.744　　　72–87078
ISBN 0–590–07247–1

Published by Four Winds Press.
A Division of Scholastic Magazines, Inc., New York, N.Y.
Copyright © 1975 by Robert Halmi.
All rights reserved.
Printed in the United States of America.
Library of Congress Catalogue Card Number: 72–87078
1　2　3　4　5　　　79　78　77　76　75

Haverford Public Library

Contents

Preface

SINCE A ZOO VISIT CAN BE A MARVELOUSLY stimulating experience, and since most of what people actually know firsthand about wild animals they have learned by visiting zoos, it is very important that zoos present a realistic setting. Without such a setting the observer sees really only half the scene. He sees the physical dimensions, features and coloration of the animal—he knows what it looks like—but he does not get much of a clue to the animal's behavior. In fact, it is likely that the viewer's overall impression will be mistaken, because he is seeing only a counterfeit wild animal. It is the same as trying to judge humans by watching the behavior of criminals in prison cells.

In my many travels to regions where wild animals are concentrated, and in my frequent visits to zoos all over the world, I have always been aware of the necessity for reconciling the animal and his environment. Many of our better zoos today are doing just that. A few of the newer ones, in which the animals roam freely and the visitors stay in "cages" (autos or buses), come close to the idea. In examining the whole subject of zoos, I hope I can point to better ways for visitors to enjoy zoos, and better zoos for visitors to enjoy.

A good zoo is living education. To see and to wonder at the variety of God's creatures makes man mindful of his special place in the world. I hope you will enjoy the special tour in this book, and that your next visit to a real zoo will be even more rewarding.

Robert Halmi

1 ⚙ The First Zoos

MANY YEARS AGO WHEN TRAVEL WAS LIM-ited mainly to the rich and adventurous, and there were no movies or photography as we know it, wild animals were the objects of much interest and amazement. The public, both in Europe and America, knew of lions and elephants, giraffes and hippos, primarily through old stories and legends. The illustrations that accompanied these stories were, for the most part, very crudely drawn. So the beasts remained mysterious, and much feared.

It is very difficult for a child today to imagine how ignorant children a century or two ago were about these animals. Even adults of that time knew very little more about the subject than children did. In Europe, on the rare occasions when a leopard was brought from Africa or a tiger from Asia, these astonishing beasts were usually offered as special gifts to kings or powerful nobles. The animal became a royal favorite, was fed the finest foods and fussed over by members of the court, who were often the only ones allowed a glimpse of it. There was seldom a place where the average person could see these prized pets, much less the hundreds of other less notable or rarer species that were not brought back alive.

Kings and emperors prided themselves on owning such marvelous and rare creatures. Long before the days when the Roman emperor Nero sat his pet tigress beside him at the dinner table, Egyptian pharaohs and Chinese princes maintained menageries in special parks or gardens. The cheetah became a favorite of aristocrats because it could be trained to hunt for them. Ownership of exotic animals, and the power to train them to some extent, was a matter of considerable pride among ancient rulers.

The Bible records that King Solomon kept monkeys and peacocks; and when Daniel was consigned to the lion's den, these were certainly beasts belonging to the royal menagerie, since King Nebuchadrezzar of Babylon was famous for his lion collection. Half a world away, in 1200 B.C. or thereabouts, a Chinese emperor maintained what was called "A Garden of Intelligence." Located next to his palace, the Garden contained specimens of nearly every wild creature that existed within the bounds of the Empire. Early Egyptian rulers sent expeditions to the south of their kingdoms to bring back wild animals for the royal enclosure. A stone in the British Museum records the exploits of King Ashur Akbar of Nineveh, leader of an expedition to capture wild animals. Inscriptions on this stone tell how each beast was put in a compound, and "by each was its name placed"—obviously for the education of the king's loyal subjects, who previously had little idea what the creatures looked like.

Aristotle, the famous Greek philosopher and tutor of

Alexander the Great, kept a sort of private zoo which was stocked at his request by Alexander's soldiers. He was possibly the first man to study animals in order to learn from their appearance and behavior. Several animals still have names of Greek origin. The word *hippopotamus* comes from Greek and was compounded from two words—*hippo* for horse and *potamus* for river. Since so little was known about jungle animals in those days, it is easy to understand how travelers tried to describe the hippopotamus to the folks back home. They probably described its resemblance to a horse— its four legs and broad back—but noted that it lived in a river. Hence the creature became catalogued as a river-horse, or hippo-potamus.

The Romans in their many battles in Asia and Africa regularly seized wild beasts as spoils of wars and displayed them in their triumphal processions. It is recorded that Emperor Augustus in 29 B.C. had a collection of 420 tigers, 260 lions and 600 African animals including cheetahs, panthers, elephants, a hippopotamus, a rhinoceros and 36 crocodiles. The Romans also kept hundreds of caged wild beasts to be used in the arena for gladiators to fight, or for shows in which the deliberately starved beasts attacked each other.

Wherever a civilization flourished, its sovereigns kept wild animals both as symbols of their power and as a means of amusement. The Great Caliph of Baghdad, Haroun-a-Raschid, who is famous in the *Arabian Nights*, had one of the largest private collections ever assembled. In the year 797 A.D., the caliph, hearing of the European ruler Charlemagne's interest in wild beasts, dispatched several monkeys and an elephant to him from Mesopotamia. As this cargo moved toward its

A print from the fifteenth or sixteenth century depicting lions confined in a palace courtyard in Florence, Italy.
NEW YORK PUBLIC LIBRARY PICTURE COLLECTION

destination, it passed through Egypt, and the Emir of Cairo added a few lions, bears and antelope to the shipment. Charlemagne was delighted by these unusual presents.

History records that Charlemagne sent the lesser beasts to compounds at his various estates, but the elephant, named Abul Aba, became his best prized possession. Travel anywhere on land was difficult in those days, but travel with an elephant was something only a great emperor would attempt. Yet for years, everywhere Charlemagne went, Abul Aba padded along behind him. Abul Aba had his own retinue of keepers, and was treated with much of the same respect that the ancients gave to the animals which were religious symbols. Although nothing was known about the scientific care of animals in those days, wild animals were probably treated even better than they are today, and much better in fact than most people were treated. Since the beasts belonged to mighty rulers, nothing was too good for them, and their keepers probably feared for their lives if anything should happen to these treasures.

In the thirteenth century, King Henry III of England amassed a sizable collection of beasts. He housed them in the Tower of London, and charged the people of London for their upkeep. This made the animals very unpopular. Instead of becoming an attraction, they were considered a nuisance. When the king was given a polar bear, to save money the keeper took the bear on a chain to the Thames River where it could fish for its own food. Then in 1254, a "miraculous" event occurred —the arrival of the first elephant ever seen in England. This, too, was added to King Henry's menagerie, but this time the public's curiosity got the better of its pocketbook. People came from all over England to see the astonishing elephant, to marvel at its size and its tusks. The City of London had to pay even more money to shelter the visitors as well as to build a suitable enclosure for the elephant. Later English rulers, including Henry VIII and Queen Elizabeth I, kept up the royal menageries, using the animals to entertain important visitors by staging combats between lions and tigers.

The English collection, however, was minor compared to the elegant establishment of the seventeenth century which Louis XIV of France built for his wild beasts adjacent to his palace at Versailles. Louis XIV is generally credited with having planned the first real zoo. He had special cages built amid the shrubs, trees and gardens, so that the landscape was harmonious

The nineteenth-century zoological garden in the Bois de Boulogne in Paris. NEW YORK PUBLIC LIBRARY PICTURE COLLECTION

and people could walk in a leisurely manner around the grounds, pausing to admire clusters of animals at various turns.

The practice of giving animals as special gifts to a sovereign or a nation has continued to the present day. When Nikita Khrushchev visited England in the early 1960s, he presented a Russian bear cub to Princess Anne. This tradition probably goes back to earliest Biblical times when Pharaohs and Persian kings prized such gifts.

Probably the most elaborate ceremony for a gift animal occurred in China in 1414, when the Emperor Yung-lo received a giraffe as a gift from a newly crowned Indian king. It happened that a Chinese merchant ship had put in at Bengal, India, and the officers of the ship had become very excited when they saw, in the king's coronation procession, long-necked creatures with the body of a deer and the tail of an ox. Oddly enough, such creatures were considered omens of good luck in China, although no such living creatures had ever been seen or heard of by the Chinese. Chinese emperors had long maintained a menagerie of beasts from distant lands, but nothing that resembled their lucky omen. Its resemblance to the giraffe lay not only in appearance, but in name as well, since the Indian name for the real beast, *k'irin,* was almost exactly the same as the Chinese name for the mythical creature.

Hence, when reality duplicated myth and a giraffe did arrive in Peking, the capital city held a special celebration. The emperor himself came to the city gates to receive this welcome guest. There were parades, festivals, speeches and special ceremonies. Court painters drew pictures of the giraffe, and the leading poets of the empire vied in writing verses in the giraffe's honor.

Eventually, a second giraffe arrived in China from a country in East Africa, and the Chinese thereupon sent a merchant fleet to that country to open up new trade, and to get more giraffes. Thus, an important event in world commerce, as well as a voyage much longer than that of Columbus and several decades prior to his explorations, can be directly linked to the gift of a giraffe.

Nearly every major center in Europe—from Russia, where rulers kept trained bears for show and sport, to Rome, where Pope Leo X kept a sizable menagerie—had a collection of wild animals under the protection of the local sovereign. Some of these consisted of just a few exotic birds or trained bears and perhaps a herd of deer, while others boasted examples of most of the major African breeds found in zoos today. Still, these collections were not often available for public viewing but instead were maintained as fashionable toys for aristocrats.

The day of the public zoo did not really come until a few years after the French Revolution, when all the wild animals kept by the French nobility became the property of the people. Not knowing what to do with these "liberated" creatures, the French eventually sent them to the Jardin des Plantes in Paris, where there at least was space for them. In a matter of a few years, this former botanical garden was turned into a large zoological garden. This time the public was more or less cordially invited to come to see them, and to provide funds for their upkeep.

The honor of being the oldest zoo in continual operation belongs to the Schonbrunn, just outside Vienna. Officially dated as a zoo since 1751, this small, gemlike zoo garden was the private preserve of the Hapsburgs, who used it for their deer herds. Emperor Francis I decided to turn it into a formal zoo as a special gift for his wife, Maria Theresa, and he supervised its construction. It was designed as a private playground with animal cages cleverly concealed in elaborate shrubbery. Expanded now, and long since a public facility, Schonbrunn is considered by some to be the loveliest zoo in the world.

2 ❀ Today's Zoos

THE TRADITIONAL ZOO, THE KIND THAT HAS become commonplace in major cities, has a history of about one hundred years. It began when a city or an individual deeded land for the purpose of housing animals. Wild creatures that were already in private hands in the vicinity were often turned over to the new enterprise, and funds were gathered to stock the zoo with captured animals. Physically, a new zoo started with an elephant or two, a couple of lions and several specimens of local birds, amphibians, deer, wildcats, or whatever else was available.

Gradually, the zoo was enriched by private donations or public funds, and its quarters as well as its menagerie were enlarged. Cities began to vie with each other in having large zoos, and they became a matter of civic pride.

By the middle of the nineteenth century there were several large zoos in Europe. The first American zoo opened in Philadelphia in 1874, followed shortly by another in Cincinnati. The idea of city zoos, which would be maintained within a city by grants of money from that city, gradually took hold; and today most zoos around the world are the special responsibility of cities, although there are several which are supported by state governments or from a national treasury. Even so, in the United States now there are only about thirty animal compounds worthy of being called zoos in that they have a wide variety of animals and spacious areas for displaying them.

It is important to keep in mind that nearly all zoos started with ample space for their original stock. Most had additional space for expansion. Consequently, there was no appreciable overcrowding until zoos tried to become "Noah's Arks"—to display pairs of practically every creature.

At this point, zoos frequently became the victims of urban expansion and population growth. Their locales, usually at the city's edge 50 years ago, became engulfed by housing and industry. In most cases, additional land adjacent to the original sites became very costly, if it could be bought at all. Hence, city zoos were hemmed in between expanding collections and limited space. The result was overcrowding; more and more animals occupied proportionately less space. Meanwhile, crowds increased, and additional footage had to be reserved for walkways, roadways, refreshment stands, lavatories and the like.

The public, it must be mentioned, came to a zoo mainly to look at animals or to spend a few leisurely hours in open spaces. They were satisfied with conditions. It is only in recent times that there has been an outcry against zoos as institutions. The animals were fed, housed, displayed and catalogued, the grounds were kept clean, and little else seemed to matter. News-

A nineteenth-century bear pit in Berne, Switzerland.
NEW YORK PUBLIC LIBRARY PICTURE COLLECTION

papers duly heralded births and new arrivals, and the zoo achieved a cultural status akin to a museum. Generally speaking, the older the city, the more crowded its zoo is likely to have become. In the United States, the East has the most crowded, the Mid-West second most populous, and the Far West seems to be catching up rapidly.

Now, it is a rare "city zoo" that does not have at least three hundred wild creatures in its confines. Most zoos have a "monkey house," a herpetorium (snake house), a lake or pond for birds, several steel-bar cages for lions, tigers, leopards and other cats, an elephant compound, a pool for polar bears, some pens for antelope and deer, lesser carnivores, plus black bears, and usually hippos, rhinos, camels, giraffes, zebras, yaks, llamas, ostriches and assorted others. The zoo may occupy as little as twenty-four acres, as it does in Fort Worth, Texas, or sprawl out for miles, as it does in San Diego. European zoos tend to be smaller in area than American ones, although there are notable exceptions, especially around London. Some Japanese zoos are like miniatures.

It is important to keep in mind that until the past century or so, man often considered that abusing animals was a sort of sport. It was considered fun to taunt animals in cages and to observe their helpless rage. Animal fights to the death were a major attraction, as were chases by dog packs. Such practices have largely been eliminated (except for events such as cock fights and fox hunts). Today, no zoo would allow its animals to be mistreated. However, public sympathy and concern for well-treated animals in cages is a new turn in human understanding. It is based on the idea of unfair-

The monkey house of the Philadelphia Zoo in the 1870s. A monkey house is still a common feature of many city zoos.

NEW YORK PUBLIC LIBRARY PICTURE COLLECTION

The interior of the Philadelphia Zoo as it appeared around 1880. Opened in 1874, it was the first American zoo.

NEW YORK PUBLIC LIBRARY PICTURE COLLECTION

ness to animals, more so than cruelty to animals. It also involves a keener appreciation by humans of the psychology and physiology of wild creatures.

Of course, most people today have visited a zoo and seen lions, antelope, apes, tigers and so on at fairly close range. Through movies and television, the public has become increasingly familiar with the actions and appearance of all kinds of creatures. Species once considered rare or exotic, such as polar bear and giraffe, now are prominently displayed in most zoos. This has led to competition to obtain specimens of rare breeds, like pandas, okapi, loris and the giant lizards of Borneo. Zoos now not only pride themselves on their facilities and the quantity of creatures they have, but also on the rareness or uniqueness of certain inhabitants.

This pursuit of rare breeds is often unfortunate because it tends to reduce further already scant wild populations. Furthermore, it produces something similar to the "star system" in movies, in which one or two animals get all the publicity and the rest are largely ignored. In the race for publicity and public support, zoo supervisors too often concentrate on importing exotic specimens and giving them prime display space. This sometimes works against the welfare of the less exotic creatures and tends to cramp a zoo's facilities. A few animals attractively presented in a realistic approximation of their natural habitat are worth far more attention than a great variety of beasts in small, smelly cages.

However, there is little chance that the city zoos of America will close in the foreseeable future. Zoo managers certainly are aware of their problems and the change in public attitude. It seems likely that city zoos will gradually change their exhibition patterns, and begin to emphasize research as much as display.

Recorded lectures will be placed next to cages, and there may be audio-visual slide films or movies which will give the viewer a comparison between the three hundred animals and their counterparts which are still roaming wild. Equipped with scientific information, these cage sideshows will help to make up for the element of natural environment which is still quite limited in city zoos, and the casual visitor will come away with a keener appreciation of the animals he has seen.

3 ❃ Bad Zoos

To UNDERSTAND WHAT A GOOD ZOO IS, WE should perhaps start by describing what a really bad zoo is. The worst zoos (which are really more like roadside attractions for passing motorists) are to be found in parts of Florida, in southern California, in desert regions of the Southwest, and in scattered places where tourist traffic provides the residents' main livelihood. Generally, these are animal "prisons," where the inmates, which range from lizards to bears, are treated like criminals of the worst sort. Some states, notably Florida, recently have passed strict laws to prevent this kind of abuse. The creatures in these compounds are often brutally treated and are kept in pens not much bigger than the animal itself. Futhermore, if they can be taught any sort of trick to coax coins from visitors, they are often kept on the verge of starvation so that they will readily perform tricks over and over in hopes of getting food as a reward. Other cases involve whip-training animals, so that they act out of fear, cowering even at the sight of a whip.

Unfortunately, examples of these abuses abound. In

This mountain lion's cage, barely large enough for the animal to turn around in, is an example of the deplorable conditions found in most roadside zoos.

Florida alone, in 1971, I noticed the following examples: A 350-pound wild boar, maintained by Indians along Florida's Tamiami Trail, was kept in a pen not big enough for the boar even to turn around in. In a so-called Dog Land, the sickly looking animals were kept in overcrowded cages and seemed to be on the verge of starvation. A mountain lion was housed in a small, smelly cage infested by flies and without any protection from the sun. Alligator pits which were just mudholes are used for alligator wrestling, in which the handler makes a few dollars from tourists in applying wrestling holds to the enfeebled 'gator. And a small elephant housed in a shabby shack was hampered by leg irons to keep it from moving more than a few feet.

Most of these abuses should have been corrected by now, since the state has issued detailed rules that describe minimum cage space for a menagerie. For example, a black bear's cage must be 20 feet long, 10 feet wide, and 10 feet high, and must include a shallow pool large enough for the bear to lie in. The habitat prescribed for a pair of large South American monkeys, must be at least 6x6x7, and must be furnished with perching areas and parallel bars. Also, no one can display a wild animal without the state's approval of habitat conditions. If the same rules went into effect everywhere, many pitiful cases of animal abuse would be avoided.

Fortunately, such abuses are limited to a few callous operators. However, several of our public zoos are a disgrace, and the cruelty they inflict is far worse because these zoos have large collections of wild creatures, are amply supported by public funds and often are the most heavily visited. One of the worst of these is right

This "wishing well" houses alligators in its small, dirty pool.

in the middle of the largest city in the United States, and it is a prime example of an animal slum. The Central Park Zoo is located right in the middle of Manhattan, and hundreds of thousands of people stroll through it each year.

In this zoo, for instance, polar bears occupy cages that consist mainly of granite boulders, are often unshielded from the blazing summer sun, and have splash pools that would hardly do for children in a backyard. Rows of antelope and other hoofed mammals are kept in narrow wire pens with floors of concrete slabs. The creatures are constantly subjected to noise and abuse from children and cranks, and food that is bad for them is continually tossed into their cages. Altogether, the zoo resembles a cellblock for criminals, with small, mostly barren cages separating the inmates, and a few isolation areas, like a monkey house, which seem to be set up to house hardened offenders.

The Central Park Zoo was built in 1934 when people knew little and cared less about proper conditions for animal display. And it has virtually no possibility for expansion because of limited available space. However, the New York Parks Department at last is becoming sensitive to criticism and has embarked on a program that will help to ease some of the zoo's intolerable conditions. Because it cannot find proper facilities, the Central Park Zoo is trading some of its larger specimens, such as hippos, camels, an orangutan and a yak, for smaller creatures that will fit into planned environment areas. Various kinds of deer will be able to roam together in the new setup, although their decorative vegetation will be made of plastic to keep them from eating it.

This polar bear in New York City's Central Park Zoo must live in a barren 20 x 30-foot cage that affords virtually no shelter from the sun.

These zebras of New York City's Central Park Zoo must spend the winter confined in a cage measuring only 15 x 20 feet.

Remarked the Parks official in charge, "Conditions once considered tolerable for animals are now being questioned." This may be the understatement of the year when applied to the Central Park Zoo, but at least New York is trying to do what it can. In trading animals with other zoos, the zoo is following the important principle of displaying fewer animals in its limited space, and trying to display these as effectively as the terrain allows. It is even more important that the head of the Parks Department realizes, and expresses, the central issues involved. He agrees that "Man is part of nature, and part of ourselves is imprisoned with the animal in the cage. For children, there is nothing educational in gaping at a miserable, caged animal. Instead, it's a dehumanizing experience."

While the Central Park Zoo has been one of the worst offenders, it is by no means alone. The methods of animal display in the Denver Zoo leave much to be desired, and there are not enough safeguards to keep the public from abusing the animals. The Audubon Park Zoo in New Orleans, though improving, is still too noisy and some of its display areas are primitive. Many other city zoos are in the same class for one reason or another, and most of them need a lot of rebuilding to come up to acceptable standards of humane treatment and educational advantage.

4 ✸ From Wild to Tame

IF WE CAN ASSUME THAT ONE-HALF OF ALL ZOO
animals are brought into captivity from a wild state,
rather than being born in a zoo, then the problem of
how to coax the wild animals to accept their new surroundings becomes very important in zoo management.
The proportion of wild-to-captive animals in zoos is, of
course, much higher for the so-called "exotics," a term
used to describe rare or unusual species, such as the
loris, the tapir, the okapi, the black-footed ferret, and
many kinds of birds and snakes, to mention just a few.
These exotics usually are costly; and since they come
from distant places and less is known about their
habits and care, the risk of early death is very high.
Also, they rarely breed in captivity because of shyness
or lack of suitable mates, so new ones are constantly
needed.

In their treatment of these exotics, which for the
most part are members of scarce or diminished species,
zoos have been guilty of the worst charge that can be
leveled against them. The death of an animal caused
by human greed or pride is the most extreme form of

cruelty. Certainly, if zoos did not compete against each other to pay high prices for exotics, the pursuers of exotics would not go to the trouble and expense of catching them. These shy creatures are hard to trap, and often die of shock, fright, or mishandling long before they can be shipped to a zoo. In fact, the humans who catch these wild animals are usually a miserable lot, unscientific in handling, unscrupulous in method and unfeeling toward their victims. These "bring-em-back-alive" operators cause more deaths of valuable wildlife than do the zoos who buy or order such species, or indeed than do all the hunters and poachers in the world put together.

Experts in the Congo have told me of gruesome cases in which mother apes are shot by hunters and their newborn infants pulled from their breasts where they were futilely trying to suck. Of three baby apes taken in this fashion, two died almost immediately and the third did not survive for more than a few weeks. The same technique of killing the mother and stealing the cubs is used for polar bears in the Arctic. It is a vicious, dirty business. This is the kind of hidden, behind-the-scenes cruelty to animals which does not show up inside zoos. No matter how pious a zookeeper may be about his menagerie, he must share the blame with some of the culprits who do his dirty work for him in deserts, jungles, mountainsides and ice floes.

Zoo-financed and -staffed expeditions to capture animals are not much better in their methods or results in the wild. Their percentage of healthy captives is of course higher, but their subsidies enable them to spend many weeks in pursuit of a single creature. Hence, they may be able to capture some rare animals which might elude the patience or skill of ordinary animal seekers. It is sickening to anyone who knows how animals are hunted and captured when he watches some of these zoo shows and episodes in movies or on television. You see the capture, and the live creature. But you will never see the victims who were maimed or killed in an attempt at capture. That film never gets out of the laboratory.

Perhaps because of the current public feeling against animal abuse, some of the captives used for television are released to roam free again. The prime purpose for tracking them down is for public entertainment. This is true despite all sorts of pious statements by the pursuers about animal research. Probably ninety percent of such activity would never take place if some humans were not making money by filming it. The question then remains—after release—whether or not the captive actually can survive the trauma of his capture, or whether the other members of his species will shun him, or even destroy him, because of the hated human scent that will cling to him for a long time.

With rare exception, wild animal capture is a nasty thing. The animals are roughly handled in the process of capture. Animal families are broken up without regard to survivors, and more animals than necessary are caught to allow for death and injury after capture. The captives are often transported in the smallest livable space, and cruelty continues until their subsequent sale or auction and delivery to a zoo. Nevertheless, the process goes on. Our zoos are stocked, and the problems of adjustment to zoo life for these wild animals must be carefully studied. Dr. H. Hediger, possibly the world's foremost expert on zoo animals, has stated that the

This young black Malayan tapir, seen here with its mother, will lose its stripes in six months. The tapir is considered an "exotic," a rare species sought by zoos for their collections. LOS ANGELES ZOO

radical change from a wild to a caged environment is equivalent to a transplant operation. This means, in effect, grafting an organ from one creature and trying to make it function properly in another. Fortunately, zoomen have a much higher success rate in "transplants" than doctors do with human hearts and kidneys.

For the most part, only young wild animals are captured for zoos. An older animal whose life patterns are firmly established can seldom be tamed or domesticated properly. The older animal has, in a sense, lost its adaptability. Its instinctive behavior is too firmly rooted and its learned responses to wild environment are too deeply ingrained to be changed. Rarely does an older animal make a suitable zoo inmate, even though it may linger in captivity for several years. Hediger speaks of death from "psychological causes" for such creatures. Their constant state of nervous anxiety makes them more prone to disease; and they often refuse all food. They lie about their cages morosely, dying sometimes from general debility (weakness) caused by the drastic change in their existence.

Younger wild creatures, however, usually survive the transition nicely. There is no exact rule for determining when an animal is too old to be restrained, but an expert guess would put the limit at no more than one-sixth of the creature's normal life expectancy in the wild. Prior to sexual maturity probably would be a better criterion. For instance, an adult moose will never be comfortable in captivity, while its young almost always will.

5 ✿ Escape

SEVERAL YEARS AGO AT A ZOOLOGICAL GAR-
den in Berne, Switzerland, a keeper accidentally left
open the gates of the deer enclosure. More out of curiosity than dissatisfaction, the herd of deer, some twelve
in all, wandered out. Shying away from noise or crowds,
they ambled toward a dense wood only a few hundred
feet from their enclosure. In this wood there lived wild
herds of the same species.

Free at last, the deer could find ample food and the
company of their own kind. Recapture was almost impossible. Yet, within a few days all of the former captives returned to their pens voluntarily. None of the
wild deer returned with them.

From this incident, and many similar ones on record,
zoo experts have concluded that captivity is not neces-
sarily hostile to the nature of wild creatures. Certainly
those beasts born and raised in captivity cannot be
said to have the same longing for freedom and wildness as those which have actually experienced it. In
fact, some leading students of animal behavior are
firmly convinced that animals which have spent their
lives in captivity never feel like prisoners, as people

Animals that enjoy considerable freedom, like these bears in the San Diego Zoo, are less inclined to seek escape than those confined to small, smelly cages.

suppose they do. Because they have never known wildness, these animals simply cannot believe that their cages or enclosures are barriers to a lost freedom. To say otherwise is to put human ideas in animal minds. It is to say that *our* thoughts are *their* thoughts. That is ridiculous.

It has been noted in nearly all zoos that creatures which have had experience in the wild and are then introduced to captivity frequently try to escape. It is popularly supposed that this reaction represents a longing to return to the idyllic existence from which they were snatched. Again, the experts take a different view. They believe that, in most instances, it is the presence of man and all the sights, sounds and smells that go with man's world which cause the animal to want to flee. Instinctively and through experience perhaps, nearly all wild animals recognize that man is an enemy. Hence, the urge to flee arises from a desire to escape a mortal enemy—man! This desire largely disappears when an animal changes his mind about man's being an enemy. That is the point at which the animal becomes tame.

Depending upon the particular species, its cage and its care, the taming process can take months, or years, or never really work. For the larger and more common mammals in zoos, such as deer, antelope, various canines and felines, elephants, rhinos, hippos and so on, it seems to work within a year. Gradually, they lose the desire to escape. Principles of behavior, human or animal, are not an exact science like physics; exceptions always occur, yet they do not disprove the rule that kindness, familiarity and adaptation bring contentment.

Animals newly brought from wildness to zoo cages

Horned animals, like these mountain goats, wishing to escape from
confinement may use their horns to get through gates or chains.

often panic because of their new surroundings. Since they do not comprehend that bars and wires are there to prevent their escape, they often lunge headlong at these barriers. They view these barriers as some sort of bush or vine growth which they can crash through. Some of them get as much of a running start as the cage allows and go banging full force against steel bars. Injury and even death result. For this reason, zookeepers resort to padded cells for some animals in their first weeks of captivity, or they confine the animal to so small a cage that it cannot get up enough speed to harm itself. This may appear cruel, but less so, surely, than a fractured skull or broken neck.

In almost all cases of the attempted or successful escape of an animal from its zoo confines, the reason can be found by figuring out what the animal is trying to escape *from,* not by guessing what it might be escaping *to.* Fear and dislike of man are the chief reasons for the escape attempts of new inmates. The reason for the escape attempts of animals accustomed to zoo life is most likely bad living conditions. There may be too much light in a cage, or not enough cover to satisfy the animal's self-protective instinct. It may be too noisy, or the zoo may be feeding the animal the wrong food, and so on. It has been noted that creatures which escape for various biological reasons usually can be found in the first place nearby that satisfies the need their cage left unfulfilled. Thus, if a small furbearer escapes and is later found in a drainpipe, it is not because the creature chose a cunning hiding place, but more likely because the pipe gave him the desired feeling of security and privacy that the cage lacked. One instance of this kind should be enough to alert a modern zookeeper to the inadequacy of the original cage, both in its barriers and its setup.

A third reason for escape is the presence in the same cage or nearby of other animals, even if they are of the same species. This proximity may alarm one animal to such an extent that he constantly tries to get away. For instance, two male elk which may have fought over a doe are not likely to be good company for each other during the mating season. The loser fears the victor and wants to get away so as not to be attacked again. Also, birds and some mammals may become extremely restless during the times of year that correspond to their migratory patterns.

Animals are extremely talented in devising cage breaks. Those with sharp teeth, horns, hoofs or claws use them as tools to break wire nets, uproot floors, or even chisel through bars. Monkeys, elephants, pigs and certain antlered species become quite adept at lifting the gate bars and chains, or undoing catches. Not only snakes, but badgers and hedgehogs as well, have squeezed through spaces which seem far too narrow to permit passage. But any animal, and especially those gifted with climbing, jumping or burrowing talents, will test the quality of its enclosure if it becomes anxious or frenzied.

In larger and more modern zoos where the animals have extra room, and may be confined by walls or pits or moats (rather than four-sided cages of steel bars like a lion's cage), there is extra danger if something really upsets an animal. In one zoo, bears have been kept behind the same walls for forty years without an escape. Yet, recently, when a female bear became terrified of a sudden loud noise, she climbed over this same wall with such ease that her handlers gaped in astonishment for a few seconds before going in pursuit. Water barriers for land animals and land barriers for aquatic ones work very well, but care is required because under extreme circumstances seals can behave like mountain climbers, monkeys can swim like fish, and polar bears can soar out of water like pole vaulters. Zoos have learned the hard way that they need safety factors far beyond normal expectancy. That is why so many zoo cages seem to be built as if to hold mad dogs or rogue elephants.

A distinction should be made between cage breakers and runaways. Very rarely does an animal run away entirely from a major zoo. Runaways are usually creatures such as lions, elephants or monkeys which have been taken out of their cages for parades, television shows, circuses and the like. A circus parade of elephants once ran wild among thousands of spectators in Munich, Germany, causing panic in the whole city, hundreds of broken bones and several deaths. In Leipzig, Germany, in 1913, a group of lions got loose from a circus caravan, causing probably the greatest urban lion hunt in history. Four were recaptured, but the police shot eight. During the pursuit, the city was virtually a ghost town, hardly anyone daring to walk the streets. In 1933, a panther on the loose from the zoo in Zurich, Switzerland, set off a tremendous public outcry, and it was not caught until ten weeks after it vanished from its cage. Of course, the more hubbub, the more dangerous the animal becomes. It feels menaced by strange sounds and sights, and its instinct for flight turns into an instinct for self-defense. Such extreme possibilities, however, cause little concern in well-managed zoos.

6 ✸ Feeding

W HEN IT COMES TO EATING, CHIMPANZEES show food preferences that are highly similar to man's. For a long time it was believed that chimpanzees, like gorillas, were vegetarians. Yet, Jane Goodall reported seeing a chimp kill and eat a mammalian prey in the Gombe Stream Game Preserve of Tanganyika. It has been found that some chimpanzees in captivity will take meat freely while others will not touch it, and in some zoos the chimps are perfectly content with a diet of fruits, vegetables, cereal, powdered milk, salt, and mineral and vitamin supplements.

There have been some instances when an animal's diet changed drastically after it moved from the natural state to the zoo. This was dramatically demonstrated by the aardvark, the ant- and termite-eating mammal from Africa, that found its way to the Bronx Zoo (New York Zoological Park) in 1949. It was fed a mixture of finely ground raw meat, coddled eggs, pablum and reconstituted evaporated milk, with vitamin concentrate added. After a while, dried ants' eggs and dried flies were added, but this food, which the aardvark had relished

A chimpanzee in Lion Country Safari.

in the wild, was ignored in captivity. When the zoo imported a quantity of dried locusts from South Africa to be added to the aardvark's diet, the animal showed no interest. The aardvark apparently knew a good dish when it was served to him and was no longer content with the old scraps.

As a rule, zoo lions do not seem to care too much what is fed them, just as long as it is red meat. Yet, a lion that becomes used to a certain type of meat can prove difficult. Some will refuse to eat liver and kidneys, and in many zoos when the fare has changed from beef to less expensive horsemeat, the lions usually protested by fasting for some time before accepting the new diet.

Generally speaking, the higher the animal is on the evolutionary scale, the harder it is to find the proper diet for him, since the foodstuffs the animal likes or needs more closely resemble man's own varied menu. While meat is the mainstay of most carnivores, and various grains and browse (stems and leaves of trees and shrubs) satisfy hoofed creatures, the diet problem becomes more complex for primates.

Below is an example of how one primate, in this case an orangutan, was fed from infancy (age 1 year, weight 10 lbs.), to the growing boy state (age 3, weight 30 lbs.), to full adulthood (age 9, weight 225 lbs.). Experts have learned that in order to be sure such an ape gets enough of what he needs, extra food must be supplied so he can pick and choose. Apes waste a lot of food, but if they do not have it to waste, malnutrition seems to result. Only humans, apparently, raise their young with the idea that they must accept what they are served and "clean their plates." Nature prefers a smorgasbord.

Here is the diet and feeding schedule of the orang-utan as a one-year-old:

8:30 A.M.   5 heaping tsp. of precooked baby cereal, plus 3 drops multiple vitamin concentrate, in 2 cups whole milk

11:00 A.M.   1 cup tomato or orange juice

1:00 P.M.   strained vegetable or baked potato, 1 apple, orange or banana, 1 slice of bread

4:30 P.M.   3 tsp. precooked cereal baby food in 1 cup whole milk, with 1 fresh egg (poached, soft-boiled or raw), on Mondays, Wednesdays and Fridays

As a three-year-old, he ate:

8:30 A.M.   1 pt. reconstituted evaporated milk, to which were added 10 drops multiple vitamin concentrate, 1 tsp. cod liver oil, ½ tsp. dicalcium phosphate, 1 poached egg, 1 tbs. honey and ¾ cup precooked baby cereal

11:00 A.M.   2 carrots, ½ stalk celery, ¼ head cabbage, 2 raw white potatoes, 3 beets

3:00 P.M.   3 bananas, 2 apples, 2 oranges, ¼ lb. grapes, 3 slices raisin bread

5:00 P.M.   Same as 8:30 A.M.

As an advanced adult:

8:30 A.M.   3 qts. milk mixture made by stirring into a small quantity of water 4 level tsps. powdered milk, 3 poached eggs, 1 tsp. cod liver oil, 1 tbs. Karo corn syrup, 1 tsp. salt, 4 oz. precooked baby cereal, ½ tsp. dicalcium phosphate and 10 drops multiple vitamin concentrate. Water was then added to make up the three quarts.

3:00 P.M.	6 apples	¼ head cabbage
	3 oranges	½ stalk celery
	10 bananas	2 raw white potatoes
	3 carrots	1 raw sweet potato
	¼ head lettuce	2 slices raisin bread

Also scattered green beans, spinach, grapes, pears and melons when available, and two handfuls of monkey pellets

5:00 P.M. 3 qts. milk mixture, as above, but minus vitamin drops

Again, it should be noted that not all this food was eaten; a lot was picked at or brushed aside. But if this quantity and an equal variety had not been set out, then the orangutan would have gone hungry or suffered a nutritional deficiency. It costs a lot of money for food and caretakers, so zoos do not like to waste anything. They do not provide daily banquets for animals, but try to carefully limit their intake to what is essential. If this one ape is multiplied by the hundred or more large animals in a sizable zoo, with all their dietary needs—from raw meat for lions, and fish for seals, to hay for elephants, and certain insects for small animals—then the difficulty of feeding a zoo collection becomes quite apparent. Furthermore, regularly scheduled feedings are important to the animals' temperaments, so this great variety of food must be set out for them on a fairly rigid schedule.

Visitors are no help in feeding animals. Regent's Park Zoo in London stopped all feeding of animals by the public in 1968. What had been happening to their

Approximately one quarter of the deaths of zoo animals are a result of the junk food and paper fed to them by visitors. These elephants were photographed at the Bronx Zoo in New York City.

elephants was one good reason for their action. William Crompton, head keeper of elephants there, reports that his elephants used to have stomach trouble after every summer weekend when crowds thronged the zoo. It took the rest of the week to cure their stomachaches, and then the next weekend it started all over again. Mr. Crompton counted 908 items of food offered to just one elephant over a period of four hours on an August afternoon! In addition, he noted that the elephant stole seven inedible items, including an umbrella—which fortunately it did not eat. Many of the food items, like candy bars, gum and picnic sandwiches, still had the wrappers on.

This was bad enough, but keeper Crompton also noted that the elephants learned to crowd the rim of their large paddock, in order to thrust out their trunks, like beggars, to the people across the protective barriers. One elephant he watched moved only about thirty feet during a whole hour. The same elephant, after public feeding was prohibited, walked hundreds of yards around the enclosure during the same hour on a following week. Furthermore, the elephant went into the pool provided for it, then rolled in sand, picked up its play log and tossed it in the air, and went through several other interesting antics. The exercise was far better for the elephant's health, and it also gave the public considerably more to watch.

Except in cases where a zoo sells packages of special foodstuffs to be offered to certain creatures, it is almost always a very bad idea for a visitor to feed anything to an animal. The food will not do the animal any good and the possibility for harm is great. You will be doing everyone a favor if you do not try to feed anything to animals, except where a zoo gives specific permission.

7 ❀ Training and Conditioning

MANY ZOO CUSTODIANS THINK IT IS IMPORtant to try to train animals. Food is usually the key to training wild animals to perform tricks, after they have become tame. Giving food as reward for a "correct" action, or withholding it as punishment for not performing the correct movement, is a tactic that seems to work as well on chimpanzees or bears as on dogs and mice. Sometimes, the result can be a series of amusing public shows, such as the one put on by chimps in the St. Louis Zoo; and sometimes it can be only a few simple motions, such as the way an elephant lifts up his trunk or a seal jumps to catch a fish. If no attempts to train zoo animals are made, some develop bad habits out of boredom, and nearly all major animals develop quirks of behavior in zoos. Some go unnoticed; others are all too easily noted. At the Zoological Gardens of London, a chimpanzee in a cage with little to occupy itself made a habit of throwing sand or small stones at spectators. Every time the chimp would make a move to throw, the visitors would duck. After stones and sand were taken out of the cage, the chimp would spit at the visitors, and finally the zoo had to place a protective pane of glass in front of the enclosure.

Public amusement, however, is considered a secondary reason for training animals. The primary purpose behind training attempts is to reduce the boredom of captivity. Thus, if the animal learns a few tricks and keepers try to teach new ones, it helps to stimulate the animal's senses. Experts feel it makes the animal more lively and less prone to sulk.

Of all the animals a zoo can boast of, the gorilla is usually the main attraction. Because of its close resemblance to humans, the gorilla seems to evoke endless public fascination. Gorillas also have brains believed to be at least equal in capacity to those of chimps. Yet, it used to be considered virtually impossible to teach gorillas to perform stunts. They just did not show any interest. However, in the Nagoya, Japan, zoo, the keeper has managed to turn his three gorillas into a performing troupe who give a couple of daily shows. They shuffle out to an exposed area, then go through the routine of having a tea party, wearing party hats and sitting at a table. When one gorilla acts naughty, the others chase him around, scolding him. Then they do a little dance and the show is over. Not much, perhaps, but certainly unusual for zoo animals.

Another instance of gorilla training occurred in a Swiss zoo, where a young ape was painstakingly trained to ride a bicycle. The ape gradually became fascinated by this toy. He began to want to practice, and he became very nervous before each public show of his riding skill. After a few performances, it became obvious that show business was bad for his health. He suffered a serious weight loss, and the keeper decided to call off the act. In a short time, the gorilla regained the lost weight and his normal disposition returned. No further attempts were made to train him.

Relatively few zoos have beaver colonies, although these valuable rodents are very popular with the public when their activities can be observed. To watch beavers cut down a tree by gnawing through the trunk or to see them busily building a dam is a delightful pastime. But zookeepers have been bothered for years by trying to find a way of giving captive beavers some kind of natural environment. Since a beaver home has to have running water, as well as foliage and mud, it is almost impossible to prevent the beavers from building a dam. When they do so, the water flowing in fills up the pond like a bathtub. Instead of running out the drainpipe, it overflows the rest of the enclosure and fouls up the whole area. Also, beavers tend to be nocturnal workers. The result of their labors can be seen, but seldom the work in progress.

Hence, beavers have not been popular with zoos, even though the public likes them. The Detroit Zoo solved the problem by putting them in a concrete enclosure where they could find no materials with which to build a dam. The beavers were also fed by hand so that they came out in daylight at a cue from their keeper. In a short time, they became daylight attractions.

Despite everything that has been discovered about the gorilla, this animal still remains the subject of many myths, as a powerful beast who spreads terror through the jungles and likes to abduct women. Actually, nothing is further from the truth. Gorillas, which grow to be over four hundred pounds in the wild and some-

Visitors to the San Diego Zoo may find this bear an amusing animal.

times over five hundred pounds in captivity, actually are shy in the presence of humans. In the natural state they do not rate as killers. The common practice of breast-thumping, often misinterpreted as an expression of rage or defiance, has been found to be really the gorilla's way of displaying its sense of well-being and contentment.

When raised from an early age in zoos, many gorillas develop a great dependency on their handlers which they carry into adulthood. Oka, a female of about eighteen months, was brought to the Bronx Zoo in 1941 with a companion, Makoko, a male of about two years of age. Both showed great timidity on their arrival, but eventually gained confidence from the soothing assurances of their keeper. Yet whenever the gentler Oka became startled, she sought comfort in the arms of Makoko, who rapidly took on the role of her male protector. Ten years later, however, Makoko met a tragic end when he lost his balance along the edge of the moat and toppled into water less than six feet deep. The gorilla made no successful attempt to swim or to seize the cables running along the side of the moat under the water as protection in the event of such an emergency. Rescuers were on the scene within minutes, but it was too late to save Makoko. After the tragedy, Oka became more dependent on her handlers.

The relationship between an animal and its handlers is usually delicate and often unpredictable. Zookeepers are well aware that an animal sometimes will react in different ways to two handlers who have the same experience and skills. In the Basle, Switzerland, zoo, the elephant Madi accepted only three keepers in its lifetime. If anyone else tried to take over the job, the pachyderm would trumpet menacingly. An ibex there objected to a new assistant keeper and stubbornly used its horns to block his way to the feeding shed. Over the years, zoos have learned to adopt a philosophical attitude toward the attractions and aversions which animals show their keepers. If they do not hit if off from the start, the zoo simply will seek a new combination.

When an animal takes to a trainer, it usually remains loyal to him, occasionally defending him against the attacks of other animals. In the Berlin Zoo, Toto, a chimpanzee, successfully defended his keeper against the more powerful Bobby, a gorilla living in the same cage. There are also instances in which the animal becomes surprisingly timid, taking refuge behind its keeper. In a cage where bears and lions were kept together, the bears sought protection from the lions by moving to the side of their trainer.

Another widely held misconception about gorillas is the notion that swings and similar devices are needed for their development while in captivity. At one period, Makoko and Oka spent a lot of time playing with hammocks made of heavy chains, but later they lost interest and the devices were removed. A female mountain gorilla in the Bronx Zoo managed to make a swing out of chains and a metal crossbar. One day while climbing the chains, she managed to get them twisted around her neck and was barely saved from death by her keepers. After that, she stayed away from the contraption and it was removed. Yet, a young male gorilla of the Zoological Gardens in London, would swing happily and freely from a rope at the top of his cage. He especially liked to twist the rope around tightly so that as it uncoiled it would spin him around as he hung on. How-

African elephants in France's Thoiry Game Park. Zookeepers often find that elephants in captivity are among the most difficult animals to handle.

ever, it is generally felt that his facility in handling ropes was exceptional for a gorilla.

The chimpanzee, on the other hand, is quite adept at climbing and leaping. For this reason, its outdoor quarters have to be carefully planned. In the Bronx Zoo in New York, for example, perpendicular walls ten feet high and fourteen feet across a shallow moat have successfully contained most of the chimps. However, when the zoo obtained a big male named Jimmy, officials cautiously decided to keep him indoors. Jimmy came from the St. Louis Zoological Park where he had been the main headliner in the troupe of performing chimps. His big act was to stand on the back of one of a circling line of cantering ponies, leap high into the air and turn a complete somersault, alighting feet first on the back of the following pony. The zoo had no wish to test its walls with a chimp of Jimmy's agility.

As in the case of gorillas, chimpanzees do not swim, although they do enjoy wading in the water. At the Zoological Park in Vincennes, Paris, the chimps stay cautiously away from the moat. When they approach their pool, though, they wade into the water up to chest level, but no further.

Among the most difficult animals to keep in captivity are elephants, especially the bulls, because of their tendency to become unruly in their old age. For this reason, it is sometimes necessary to destroy a zoo beast. For instance, Congo, a forest elephant, came to the Bronx Zoo in 1905. From the beginning he was ill-tempered and could be kept under control only by Alice, an easy-going Indian elephant cow who had adopted him. However, ten years later, Congo tried to impale a zoo official on his tusks, and shortly afterward was put to death by a rifle bullet. Such incidents of savage reversion still happen in the best of zoos for reasons ranging from disease to the instinctive dislike of man which no longer can be repressed. Wild animals often have motives which defy explanation by humans, and outbursts of violence that are unpredictable.

Some bulls, like the famous Jumbo, fare somewhat better in their old age. An African bush elephant, Jumbo was quite popular at the Zoological Gardens of London, where he served as a riding animal. Gradually his temper grew worse, and in 1881, when he was about twenty, he was sold to the circus of P. T. Barnum, where he achieved great acclaim. After being with the circus for about three years, Jumbo met an untimely end when he was struck by a railway locomotive at St. Thomas, Canada.

Zookeepers have noted that mature male Indian elephants in captivity are subject to periods of irritability and restlessness which cause them to wreak havoc on their surroundings and sometimes even to attack their keepers. This condition, zoo veterinarians determined, is associated with the enlargement of glands which lie between the ear and the eye and the discharge of a black, oily substance. This particular state is called "must" or "musth" and in some instances it has even been observed in females. The most effective remedy for "must" has been to cut down on the diet, limiting the animal mainly to reduced amounts of greens. Records kept by zoos show that "must" usually appears at about the eighteenth year of the elephant's fifty to sixty year average lifespan in captivity (closer to thirty-five years in the wild), and lasts only for a few years. The African male elephant in captivity, however, does not seem to go through this stage. It is believed that he is inhibited by the artificial environment.

The lion has proved to be one of the most adaptable members of the zoo community. A bold, powerful hunter in the natural state, the lion in the captive state becomes comparatively docile. A group of male lions living together without any females in the outdoor enclosure of the Bronx Zoo, after settling their differences, got along on such good terms that they eventually became too inactive and had to be dispersed.

If lions are housed in reasonably roomy quarters, pairs which are happily mated tend to live peacefully together in captivity. The female gives birth to and raises her cubs without any interference from the male, who usually take a mild paternal interest in his offspring. Unfortunately, because the lions breed so easily in captivity, a surplus of hungry cubs becomes an economic hardship for a zoo. Because of this, the sexes are usually segregated in most zoos, with breeding permitted only on occasion.

Tigers in captivity appear to be as well known to ancient man as the lion, and records show that these animals were among the tenants of the earliest zoos. While the tiger thrives inside a zoo, its lifespan (around twenty years) in captivity does not appear to be as long as the lion's (up to about twenty-nine years). In the wild, this lifespan would probably be reduced by about 40 percent due to disease, injury, infection, parasites, tooth erosion and so on. Nearly all animals live considerably longer in captivity than in the wild because of better feeding and modern veterinary medicine. Also, the tiger does not breed inside a zoo as easily as the lion. Housing conditions for tigers are about the same

Thoiry Game Park boasts the largest collection of lions in captivity.

as for lions, except that pools are generally provided for the striped beasts to satisfy their desire to frolic in the water.

While cats in general are highly adaptive to zoo living, there are instances where some have undergone unexpected changes in character, causing problems in their adjustment to captivity. This has occurred with leopards in a way to disprove the saying that they don't change their spots. Being natural water enthusiasts and swimmers like the tigers, the leopards were given a pool inside their enclosure at the Bronx Zoo. Yet, instead of having a splashing good time as was expected, the spotted beasts began behaving like domestic cats, avoiding the water and stiffly shaking their legs each time

Leopards are part of the group of major African animals displayed
at Lion Country Safari.

their feet got wet. For leopards in captivity, water has become good only for drinking.

Most zoos traditionally have provided large cats with heated quarters for winter. An exception has been the Baltimore Zoo, which mainly because of a lack of funds, has never had heated cages for cats, even though winter temperatures in Baltimore are often about 25 degrees Farenheit or below. Yet, since about 1900, this zoo has successfully maintained a thriving collection of panthers, leopards, tigers and pumas, and it can be assumed that these cats have adapted quite well to Baltimore's climate. Recently, the zoo added jaguars and cheetahs to its collection, and both species not only survived their first unheated winter without difficulty, but also seemed to enjoy the snow.

Change of attitude is not unusual with animals after they have begun living inside a zoo. This was demonstrated by a giant otter which arrived at the São Paulo, Brazil, zoo in 1955. In nature, these high-spirited animals inhabit the rivers of South America, growing to lengths of more than six feet. The São Paulo Zoo's giant otter, a female, was not fully grown when she arrived, measuring only forty-three inches in length. She was kept inside an exhibition cage where she dove and swam, and at night she was admitted to a small compartment where she slept. When she reached maturity, zoo officials felt she had outgrown her quarters and moved her to a large outdoor enclosure. The giant otter did not take well to the move. She became depressed, began whining, refused to perform or eat. She did not become her old jovial self again until her keepers returned her to the old cramped quarters.

Rhinoceroses, on the other hand, need physical help

from the zoos in order to adapt successfully to captivity. Since their horns are constantly growing, the rhinos have to have something on which to file them down. Zookeepers are constantly on the alert for sharp metal projections or gates, fences and walls on which these animals might hurt themselves. Some zoos have tried putting up a small tree stump which the rhinos can safely rub their horns against, but in many instances the animals have just ignored the stump.

Serious problems often arise during mating periods when the male and female kept together in the same enclosure play roughly with each other. To prevent the rhinos from maiming one another during lovers' quarrels, zoo officials carefully blunt the horns. After the fight ends, some of the rhinos proceed to breed successfully, while others remain unreconciled, but at least for their efforts they are left suffering nothing more than hurt feelings.

8 ❂ Touring U.S. Zoos

THERE ARE MANY INSTANCES IN WHICH CITY
zoos do a superb job. These, however, usually involve birds, reptiles, insects, amphibians, small mammals such as raccoons and several types of monkey—
in general, those creatures whose proper biosphere, or
natural habitat, can be reproduced in relatively small
areas, with careful controls of temperatures, humidity,
soil, etc. In these biospheres, often referred to unglam-
orously as snake houses, aviaries or insect worlds, a
compatible mixture of species is introduced, and the
creatures can more or less simulate their natural life
cycles under public observation.

Some of these biospheres are quite ingenious. In the
Bronx Zoo, the aquatic bird building has facsimiles of
jungle streams, marshes, cliffs, real sand, grass, and
waves washing onto beaches with the sound of roaring
surf. In this atmosphere, some aquatic birds which
never laid an egg in captivity before have begun to pro-
duce live offspring. In the National Zoological Park in
Washington there is an outdoor, free-flight cage together with natural greenery and waterfalls where you

The outdoor free-flight bird cage at the National Zoological Park in Washington, D. C. THE SMITHSONIAN INSTITUTION

The Detroit Zoo's replica of an African swamp, with crested cranes and blackbucks. DICK SIMPSON, DETROIT ZOOLOGICAL PARK

can meet cormorants, roadrunners and mynah birds, in addition to various waterfowl. The Philadelphia Zoological Garden has a marvelous hummingbird house, featuring a huge fiberglass tree from which hangs real moss. From an elevated walkway, you can watch these tiny birds whirr into action, while an electric counter reveals their fantastic wing-flapping speed. The enclosure has twenty kinds of hummingbirds, and many other small, colorful birds as well. To make the environment more naturalistic, there are fish, turtles, lizards and frogs.

In Tokyo is probably the world's most absorbing display of insect life, a treasury of fifteen thousand winged and crawling creatures living almost exactly as they would if they were not on public display under glass. Of course, many zoos boast excellent reptile houses, and there are indoor aquaria too numerous to mention, as well as outdoor aquaria such as Miami's Seaquarium, and California's Marineland of the Pacific.

All these collections and exhibits are valuable and most of them are highly instructive. Yet, major mammals are the backbone of a good zoo, and what really entertains and informs the public most are the major species of African and North American wildlife, plus a sprinkling of such species as Indian tiger and Siberian snow leopard, the South American jaguar and llama, the Chinese panda, Australian koala, Carpathian (Russian) bear, Yugoslavian chamois (stag), Arabian camel, and so on. To the extent that these creatures can be shown attractively, a zoo can take pride in its public service.

What follows here can only be a modest outline of the many excellent attractions various United States

Grant's zebras and Lechwe waterbucks on the re-created African plain at the Detroit Zoo. DETROIT ZOOLOGICAL PARK

zoos offer, but it will indicate what city zoos have been able to accomplish within their limited space and budgets.

In the Detroit Zoo are two areas of special note. One is a replica of a Lower Nile swampland, in which small antelope frolic beside flamingos, cranes and other water birds. Nearby, on a simulated African plain, the kind so familiar in Tanzania, the Detroit Zoo shows to advantage a nice herd of waterbucks and elands mingled with ostriches and zebras. Similar combinations of plains animals can be seen in Africa and, at least in summer, some shade trees allow the animals to rest under them, as they might at midday in Africa.

In Chicago's Brookfield Zoo, there is a sort of minimountain which allows the Siberian ibex to practice some of its nimble leaps among the crags. Those who see them are especially fortunate, for these creatures, like the bighorn sheep and mountain goats which inhabit high peaks in our own Rockies, put on an amazing show. In the past, the opportunity to view such animals in the wild has been limited to a few naturalists who are skilled mountain climbers.

Nearby, the Milwaukee Zoo has two areas of special appeal. One of these approximates conditions in the early stages of American development when such big fellows as moose and grizzlies shared areas with deer and birds. A combination of meadow and rocky sites allows each creature to utilize the part of the environment it naturally favors. Also, Milwaukee has continental groupings of African animals, artfully separated to keep the lions from mischief, but allowing viewers to observe the big cats at play through glass portholes. The zoo boasts one of the showings of the rare bongo ante-

Alaska moose and Alaska brown bear in the Milwaukee Zoo's area for North American animals. MILWAUKEE COUNTY ZOO

lope, which is a forest dweller but now happily shares a zoo range with rhinos and hippos.

Moving on to Oklahoma City, I thoroughly enjoyed this zoo's special area set aside for wild canines. There are Cape hunting dogs from Africa, wolves, coyotes, dingoes from Australia, Indian jackals and probably some hybrids of these species, because they interbreed freely. Each type of wild dog has a large area with vegetation found in its place of origin, and since they are well fed, there is no temptation to revert to hunting in packs.

No zoo story would be complete without a passing notice of the performing antics the St. Louis Zoological Park offers. Chimpanzees are the stars, for their riding tactics on wheeled vehicles always delight spectators. Also, the elephant show, in which the elephants play a crude form of baseball, obviously took years of patient training. There is always the question of whether such shows are educational, but in St. Louis' case it is carried out with care and gusto, and the animals seem to be in tip-top shape. Zookeepers always should try to keep their animals sufficiently stimulated so that they do not loll around their cages in total boredom. If it takes a bit of show business training to keep the animals' spirits up, it is probably a good thing overall.

The Cincinnati Zoo has three areas of special interest. Most notable is its collection of wild cats, including the only Persian leopard in the United States. While the cage settings leave much to be desired, the variety of cats (including, of course, lions and tigers) is impressive, and the zoo has had success in breeding some of the rarer species. Similarly, the zoo's black rhino breeding program has progressed to the point where it

The Milwaukee Zoo's grouping of African animals includes elands, zebras, ostriches, and lions. MILWAUKEE COUNTY ZOO

recently opened a new area to show off its homebreds. In any zoo, gorillas are sure to be hits, and Cincinnati has as cute a pair of primates as you will find anywhere. They are a male and a female, still babies really, and the zoo has great hopes for them.

Out West, the Los Angeles Zoo has been helping to keep up the world's stock of Arabian oryx, which were once plentiful across North Africa but now number a pathetic few. And of special note to zoo buffs, Los Angeles has probably the world's only complete collection of tapirs, a mixture of rhino and wild pig, native to both South America and Malaya and Sumatra. Each of the four species extant has a long, pointy snout, and the tapir's hoofs have an odd number of toes, a distinction it shares only with the horse family and the rhino. Some rare animals which seem to provide a missing link between families of creatures, like the tapir, are deserving of special display.

In the San Francisco Zoological Garden, there is an Asian environment where species of deer and antelope peculiar to that continent can roam fairly freely. This is exceptional because there are relatively few collections of Asian game, and even fewer zoo areas which attempt to match their pastureland, which resembles some of the unspoiled high plateau areas still left in America. Also of note in this zoo are the wild and wooly musk-oxen, probably the shaggiest creatures anywhere.

The Washington, D.C. zoo, which claims to have the most visitors of any zoo in the United States (about five million a year), has had a few celebrities among its menagerie, such as Smokey, the model for the fire-prevention bear, and Ham, the chimp who took a rocket ride to outer space. Altogether, this zoo is too much like a

This Australian dingo is part of the Oklahoma City Zoo's special collection of wild canines. OKLAHOMA CITY ZOO

This female Persian leopard was born at the Cincinnati Zoo in 1969. There are only a few of these rare animals in captivity in the United States.
KEN STEWART, CINCINNATI ZOO

museum, with too much attention to individual inmates and not enough attention to major animal groupings. But its water pools with pygmy hippos (whose skin may crack if they are out of water for more than a couple of hours) are delightful to observe, and any zoo that has an Indonesian dragon lizard has a real prize. This latter creature looks more like one of the smaller dinosaurs of prehistory than does any other living species.

At least two other zoos rate honorable mention on this list, although they differ from the traditional mold. The Catskill Game Farm, a leisurely three-hour drive from the center of New York City, has an incredible menagerie of nearly three thousand horned and hoofed creatures, including dozens of species of deer, antelope, goats, Mongolian ponies, llamas, asses, African cattle and so on. The farm is like one big pasture where the creatures can intermingle to some extent and there are no predators to bother them. In some ways this extraordinary Game Farm resembles what might happen if we gave the land back to the animals.

The last zoo is very limited in its scope, but is supermodern in its presentation. The Arizona-Sonora Museum in Tucson re-creates a desert environment, and if you push a button in some parts of it, you can turn on bright lights in a dark sleeping area where nocturnal animals hole up during the day. Small foxes, skunks and porcupines and vampire bat caves spring to life in a flash of light. However, they are left alone enough of the time so that their basic behavior patterns are not upset.

As pointed out, the zoo highlights here are only a modest sample of the many wonderful attractions in the United States. Almost all the zoos mentioned are supported by municipalities as adjuncts to a city's recreational program—and in some cases to its educational program too. Mainly, however, these are zoos of the present. Each has its limitations in space, money and creative possibilities. But a new type of zoo is springing up all over the world, and in time these new zoos will eclipse the old, for they have a better plan, and they have the advantage of starting fresh and learning from previous mistakes.

For a decade or two, it will not be easy for many people to visit these new zoos, certainly not like the tens of millions who visit city zoos. But in time, they will be widespread enough and will compete actively for public interest. The new zoos will also offer greater opportunity for education and research because their environments will be close to the animals' natural habitats, and the animals, at last, may find comfort and pleasure in doing things their own instinctive ways, in places where their species never set foot before.

9 ☼ Tomorrow's Zoos

THESE DAYS, ZOOS ARE UNDERGOING SUCH profound changes that within a generation or two the kinds of animal compounds that were prevalent before World War II and the improved versions that were built until about 1960 will seem like relics of a previous civilization. In the words of William Conway, Director of the New York Zoological Society, which runs the Bronx Zoo, "The term 'zoo' is already out of date." He sees modern "zoos" as environmental science centers.

This means essentially that traditional arrangements are out—no more lion cages and monkey houses, no rows of shoddy, wire pens for hoofed animals, no rhinos behind stout steel bars, no elephants behind walls. Instead, the emphasis will be on copying the animal's natural environment. Most of the better new zoos and those planned in the future will try to present their menageries within ecosystems. This involves not only open land with compatible terrain, vegetation and climate (if possible), but also includes the company of various animals that would normally share a particular range. Thus, zebras and giraffes, elands and buffalo may possibly share a zoo enclosure of several acres. They will drink at the same waterholes and feed on plants similar to those found in East Africa.

Nearby, perhaps, a pride of lions will growl ominously. As predators, they know instinctively that antelope and zebra are natural prey for them. But these targets will be shielded by deep moats which the lions cannot cross, or a fence cleverly concealed to blend with the foliage. Surprisingly, prey and predator often come into close contact in the wild, without causing alarm to the prey. The "victims" seem to sense when their foes are on the hunt and when they are merely lazing around. The difference is the food supply. Well-fed predators do not attack and zoos keep predators very well fed.

To date, no American zoo has allowed predators to earn their own food by killing and eating other inmates. This would not only be a very costly procedure, but would probably not serve any useful purpose. Since the lions or leopards or tigers are not going to be shipped back home to fend for themselves in the wild, there is no need to sharpen their hunting techniques. Also, the visiting public would not take kindly to the sight of a lion leaping onto the neck of an antelope and inflicting deadly wounds with teeth and claws. Hence, the cats or hyenas or wild hunting dogs and other predators have to be segregated into ranges where they find no natural targets to hunt.

On the other hand, it is obvious that monkeys and apes would probably not adapt to the same environment that satisfies a hippopotamus, a kangaroo or a panda. On and on go the ecological subdivisions, as mixed as nature itself. Special environments are needed for the

In contrast to small city zoos, animal preserves like Thoiry Game Park in France afford much more land on which the animals may roam freely.

polar bear and the bird of prey, for amphibians and pronghorns, for the wolf and llama. Zoos have been responding to this challenge by setting off areas to show groupings of animals. More and more research and planning have been going into these settings to make them as realistic as possible, and to display together as many animals as possible where temperaments and origins are compatible and the zoo facilities will allow.

This arrangement is indeed a great improvement— a delight for the eye of the spectator and a great advance in education since it greatly increases the viewer's appreciation of how animals actually behave. Nevertheless, such modern zoos, as improved as they may be, are still not the answer to an adequate presentation for many species. This does not really occur until the animals "own" the land and the spectators are handled like captives, with their movements carefully restricted to well-defined pathways or enclosures; or until a visitor is required to be seated in a car, bus or train.

This new concept usually requires much more land than city zoos can provide. Hence, it is hardly surprising that new zoos are moving out into the countryside. When they do this, their physical characteristics change and the zoos become more like the game preserves of Africa or India. Something else changes too, and that something is fundamental to increased education: the visitor goes to a zoo not just to see what certain animals "*look* like," but to see what these animals "*are* like."

To cite only one example—most readers of this book have seen the long-neck giraffe with its head towering above its cage barriers. A few readers have seen a giraffe bend over to pick up food held in people's hands. But how many have seen the way a giraffe actually feeds itself, by wrapping its long, sandpapery tongue around clusters of leaves in the upper branches of trees and tearing them off as if his tongue were a long scissors? This is the difference between simply seeing a giraffe, and getting an idea of how a giraffe is adapted to its natural environment. Its long neck has enabled the giraffe to survive in the wild because it allowed the animal to reach up high and eat the foliage which other animals could not reach. If the giraffe had to bend down to eat, as it does to take a peanut from a human hand, it would never have survived the competition from other herbivores.

In recent years, as the principles of ecology have become more well known, people have begun to understand that a zoo animal in close confinement really does not reveal much of its life patterns. What the viewer observes are mainly the physical characteristics of size, shape, color, and means of locomotion. What he misses are the marvelous ways each creature adapts to its environment, and in turn how it affects that environment.

Reptiles, birds and mammals are high in the evolutionary scale, but their ability to get along in the wild took many millions of years of adjustment. The simple act of grazing on grass or browsing on leaves involves very complex factors.

To glimpse a deer in the wild delicately nibbling on plant life will tell you more about the nature of deer than will a whole day of observing a zoo pen. For one thing, a wild deer never for a moment loses its instinct for caution. Its senses of smell and hearing are constantly on the alert, although it appears to be completely absorbed in eating. In captivity, these senses are not

Visitors to Thoiry Game Park see giraffes in their natural environment and may observe how the animals' unusual features are adapted
for their survival.

used. Handout feedings, removal of predators, no open season for hunters—all dull the animal. To the trained observer, something of the essence of the deer is lacking when it is caged in. There is no feeling of energy, of alertness, of the ability of instant flight. The same, in measure, is true for a tapir or a tiger, a bighorn sheep or a polar bear.

However, the fact that zoos are second best for observing animals is hardly an argument against them. For without zoos, the plain fact is that the great majority of our urban and suburban population would never see significant wildlife. They might not even see a rattlesnake or a bat. Hence, zoos have to be accounted as primarily educational institutions. The problem, then, is to make zoos better institutions for education.

10❖Setting the Trend

ALMOST WITHOUT EXCEPTION, THE ZOOS OF tomorrow are being constructed many miles from large cities, and they are being operated by private companies for profit. They receive no tax dollars, so these zoos must concentrate on showing off their animals to the greatest advantage so that people will be willing to pay admission. Since the public is paying, as well as driving many miles to see the animals, they must not be disappointed in what they see, or how they see it, or these zoos would have to close.

Hence, the new zoos tend to concentrate on relatively few creatures, usually the bigger and more glamorous African animals such as elephants, lions, hippos, rhinos, larger antelope and so on. What they lack in variety (as compared to a city zoo), they make up for by providing settings as close to nature as possible. In some of these places, lions have pretty much the run of the place, and it is, undeniably, quite a thrill to have a large lion jump on the hood of your car and peer curiously at you through the windshield. City zoos do not offer such an attraction.

About the best that can be done along old lines is demonstrated by the new Minneapolis–St. Paul Zoo, unveiled in 1974. This zoo, at least five years in the planning and building stage, is directed by Dr. Philip Ogilvie, a specialist in behavioral psychology.

Dr. Ogilvie believes that a zoo should be primarily "a classroom for environmental education." He also says that he took the job because he "didn't like zoos." What Dr. Ogilvie means is that he does not approve of the ordinary zoos around the world. He wants to change the concept, and he took a job which offers that opportunity. He wants the public to be privy to the research the zoo may conduct, and intends, for one thing, to have electronic devices fastened to hibernating bears so the public can notice their reduced heartbeat, breathing and temperature and compare these readings to those of a bear that does not hibernate.

This is only the beginning of Dr. Ogilvie's ideas. Taking advantage of Minnesota's cold climate, he has filled hundreds of acres with various cold-weather settings, such as may be found in northerly climates around the world. Each region features the animals that normally live there. The new zoo has a monorail train which allows visitors to view in comfort all the animals—moose, polar bear, beaver, caribou, and also a couple of Alaskan brown bears, the biggest member of the bear family. The zoo even has in its collection a rare snow leopard in a Himalayan setting, and the leopard is trained to leap across a chasm to get food when the monorail car approaches.

But the most important feature in the whole zoo plan is the arrangement whereby the public will be introduced to the animal's environment, not the reverse.

Theoretically, people see what they might see if they went to the actual region the zoo inmates came from. This is expected to have a beneficial effect on zoo breeding, as well as advancing the education of visitors, who hear a detailed commentary within the comfort of the zoo train. After all, there is absolutely no reason why a zoo visitor should have to undergo the rigors of an Arctic explorer just to appreciate how animals live there. He can see it and learn about it, but he doesn't have to get frostbite to complete his education.

In considering zoo patterns of the future, it is not necessary to examine in detail all the game parks that have cropped up lately—from antelope ranches in Texas

Visitors driving through either of the Lion Country preserves may find a lion cub on the trunk of their car!

to platypus preserves in Australia. We can get a broad view of the trend by looking at three major places. These are Thoiry Game Park in France; Lion Country Safari in the United States (actually two parks, one in southern Florida and one in southern California), and the remarkable San Diego Zoo, probably the finest of its kind in the world. The San Diego Zoo is included because its operation extends into new areas of zoo management, as well as incorporating the traditional ones.

To detour for just a moment, it is interesting to learn how these new zoos got their start, for they began under peculiar circumstances. The Marquess of Bath, descendant of a noble English family, inherited some nine thousand acres of land in the late 1940s, along with an inheritance tax bill for about three million dollars. The marquess had to sell most of his land to pay the taxes. Even so, there remained the problem of how to pay the upkeep on his one hundred–room castle, and care for the remaining lands. The marquess was about to go bankrupt when Jimmy Chipperfield, a circus manager, talked him into a strange partnership.

Chipperfield suggested the marquess turn his grounds into an African animal farm and charge the public admission to look around. The marquess may have thought Chipperfield was balmy, but he went along with the plan. Thus began the attraction which is known as the Lions of Longleat (the name of the marquess' ancestral realm). Several lions were imported and turned loose on the grounds, with some fences to keep them from straying. The visitors had to stay in their cars to be safe.

The novelty of it all soon brought the public in droves.

The San Diego Zoo is a pioneer in both research and animal display.

At first, there was great alarm over public safety, but this was then overcome because many thousands visited Longleat without getting a scratch. The menagerie has been increased in recent years to include several other African animals, including a twenty-foot python which loves the big, old English trees. The cash is rolling in so well that the marquess and his family can continue to live in the style they are accustomed to. The moral of this story was not lost. It was possible to put a zoo almost anywhere, and to please the public while making a profit. A new boom in zoos began, and to date the public has indeed benefited, as has, generally, the cause of preserving wildlife.

One good example of the more innovative zoos is the San Diego Zoo, founded in 1916. This zoo can show everything in the open air, which means no smelly, stuffy houses for either the animals or the public. And what this zoo shows, all within comfortable, spacious quarters, is a truly remarkable panorama of wildlife— over five thousand different creatures including some fifteen hundred kinds of mammals. Outside Australia, it is the best place in the world to observe such unique Australian species as the koala, tree-climbing kangaroo and duck-billed platypus. It also has rare, small chimpanzees, a remarkable array of colorfully plumed birds, and perhaps the world's most fascinating collection of hyenas. The latter is an animal that is grossly misunderstood and wrongfully despised because of its howl, its sloping spine, which gives it a slinky, cowardly look, and its tendency to eat carrion. Actually, in the San Diego Zoo you can get a better idea of what hyenas are like than most safari-goers do in Africa. In the zoo, the hyena comes into its own as probably the cleverest and toughest member of the canine family.

These white rhinos at the Whipsnade Zoo in Bedfordshire, England, were imported from South Africa. POPPERFOTO

The San Diego Zoo is directed by Dr. Charles Schroeder, a specialist in veterinary medicine. Discussing his remarkable zoo and some of the special work being done there, Dr. Schroeder said, "We're very much concerned with the diseases that bother animals in their native habitats. Our specialists study these diseases when an animal is brought to us, and what we learn can then be used to help the wild ones. In this way, we are helping to keep up the natural supply of wildlife. Our facilities for study of these problems are better than natural wildlife areas can maintain."

Dr. Schroeder points to a new area in his domain, the San Diego Wild Animal Park, devoted exclusively to the white rhino. Twenty-one rhinos live there, but Dr. Schroeder feels that the area, although larger than the zoo's basic one hundred–acre layout, is still too small for the large-scale breeding program he hopes for. He believes, "The day will come when we will have several hundred acres available to just a few animals."

All this is very costly, and Dr. Schroeder emphasizes that the visiting public has to pay for it, if such programs are to continue. He explains, "Zoos around the world are concerned with reproduction of endangered species. Perhaps some day we can use the animals born in zoos to repropagate wild areas. But mainly we want to be sure we maintain a breeding nucleus in zoos to perpetuate the species and to show rare animals to people. I don't think they should be hidden—even those seriously in danger should be shown to people—it's vital to education. There are many animals today that you can only see in zoos and protected parks. They can no longer exist in their original environment. The white-tailed gnu is one example."

"The San Diego Zoo operates a fleet of twenty buses and a sizable staff of guides to conduct tours through their main operation centers. Dr. Schroeder believes that this combination of personal viewing and professional explanation offers the maximum chance for entertainment and education. "The people who leave here are impressed. They have enjoyed something, they have learned something, taken some important facts home with them." He feels that a good zoo provides an opportunity for family recreation, as well as furthering the goals of education, research and public interest in conservation.

"You know," says Dr. Schroeder, "years ago miners took little canaries into the pits with them, and if the canary died from bad chemicals in the air, it was time for the miners to get out. Well, today we are seeing something like that. Because of automobile exhausts, some animals are showing high concentrations of lead. We first learned this in zoos. Maybe some of our zoo animals are our early warning system. Zoos will be among the greatest laboratories of the future."

The San Diego Zoo is pioneering in both research and animal display. Through its expanded parks, it is taking part of a city zoo out into the countryside where it can breathe—and breed. It is breaking the mold that confines many city zoos, and showing the way to a better zoo habitat for animals—and people.

Another atypical zoo is Lion Country Safari, which represents the best American plan for the display of major African animals. The fact that it has prospered in both its Florida and California settings is encouraging because every densely populated area of the United States should have such a zoo, or preserve, nearby.

Lions of Lion Country Safari.

Mr. Harry Shuster, who heads the Lion Country operations, expects to open at least six new sites in the coming years.

"There is one main reason why ordinary zoos cannot turn into our type of wildlife preserve," says Mr. Shuster. "This is the matter of land, and the cost of city land. You would need at least an additional five hundred or six hundred acres, almost a square mile, and where would you find that within a city? And how would you pay for it?"

Land is available relatively cheaply usually only outside the city, and therefore the city is not involved. Any possible wildlife preserve there then becomes a state matter, and very few states want to take an active interest in running zoos. Or, the Federal Government

might take a hand, but it has its own National Parks system, which is primarily oriented to people—for camping, hiking, etc. There are animal attractions within federal parks (and some state ones), but these areas (like Yellowstone) are too remote to attract a significant number of inner-city dwellers—the people who most need to know and understand zoos, wildlife and conservation.

What is so important about the Lion Country type of preserve is that the environment belongs to the animals —they are seen within reasonably natural settings and they are free to conduct themselves in ways closely resembling their patterns in the wild. The lion, the most popular zoo animal, comes into its own here. Families can form social units, called "prides," and visitors can actually see how mother lions raise their cubs. With patience and expert guides, they can see something else they will virtually never see in a zoo— the role of "aunts" in bringing up cubs. For lion mothers often get help from other females in the pride, and the cubs soon learn that "aunty" might play with them at times when mom would smack them if they bothered her.

This is a small point in lion behavior, but it emphasizes what such preserves can teach. Of course, you will still have to go to Africa to observe how a lion family actually hunts—with the males getting upwind of the prey so their scent will carry and frighten the prey off in the opposite direction, where the females are waiting in ambush for it! But in preserve areas where food is distributed as it is in the wild, you can see how the male eats his fill before anyone else gets anything. Then comes the female's turn, and finally, the cubs get what is left. This is how it is in nature, and that is an overriding reason why it should be known. Such matters are a thousand times more important to human understanding and appreciation of animals than all the antics of a dancing bear or a juggling seal.

Mr. Shuster takes the long-range view that operations like his Lion Country will someday be the home of all major African wildlife. He believes it is likely that there will eventually be more lions, cheetahs, elephants, rhinos, etc. in game preserves than in the wild. Indeed, it becomes more likely as Africa continues to use more of its open land to feed and house people, so that major species may be eliminated altogether from the continent, and will continue to flourish only in preserves.

This makes the role of "open zoos" even more important, because they may be just about the last places where big game can be shown in anything like its original setting. City zoos can preserve these creatures but, again, they cannot show them as they really are. A large animal species whose sole surviving members are in a few cages is little more than a replica of the vanished dinosaur which has been built out of plywood and canvas and stands in a museum.

In time, too, commercial zoos may be able to expand their concepts to take in North American wildlife, or South African or Siberian or Asian or whatever. Since these are profit-motivated organizations, if public interest is stimulated so that more and more people pay admission fees, then some of the profit will go back into expansion efforts. Allocation of taxes for expanded zoo operations is getting tighter and tighter. Hence, commercial zoos represent a new, independently financed option, perhaps the only one possible now.

Hippopotamuses have long been favored members of animal collections. It is recorded that in 29 B.C. the Roman Emperor Augustus had a hippopotamus in his collection of African animals.

Lion Country, and many others with similar plans, have shown genuine interest in breeding operations. Lion Country has successfully bred the rare addax. It is also progressing with plans for a cheetah breeding program, which is important because these graceful felines are becoming an endangered species in the wild. It has pioneered research on feeding programs for the lion and cheetah and on the social behavior of these animals. In its first year of operation in Orange County, California (near Disneyland), Lion Country drew over a million tourists.

Mr. Shuster thinks it is important for children to become aware of wildlife as living creatures. In that way, they will develop a fondness for them and an urge to help to protect them. But he feels it is even more important for adults to get this knowledge firsthand because they are the ones who have an immediate effect on programs to preserve wildlife. He does not believe zoos should be geared exclusively to children because most adults have just as much to learn and to appreciate about the value of wildlife.

Now let us take a tour through one of the best open zoos in the world, the Thoiry Game Park, located about twenty-five miles west of Paris, France, an easy thirty-five-minute drive on a superhighway. Our guide is Viscount Paul de la Panouse, son of the owner of the Chateau Thoiry, a 1,250-acre estate, with a main house of about eighty rooms, built in 1564. The house, its furnishings and archives are a tourist attraction in themselves, but, like Longleat, they cost a fortune every year just for the upkeep.

Viscount Paul needed an attraction to bring in more revenue. He considered many ideas, including a sort of

Disneyland. "But that would ruin the grounds," said Paul, "so we decided on a game park, and I spent years studying zoos around the world. Unfortunately, most of what I learned in zoos is not useful where animals roam freely. So much we had to learn for ourselves here. Of course, we did learn one thing from Longleat. When they opened on a Monday, they had forty lions. By Thursday, they had twenty. The lions had killed each other. There were fights between the tribes, the prides. We prevented that by separating our tribes at night and in the early morning feeding times, when they would be likely to fight. Now, we are able to show them together, without those ugly fences."

One of the first sights on a tour of Thoiry is the Monkey Town, a gloriously green fifteen acres of trees and bushes and lawns with winding walkways. Overhead and underfoot, dozens of monkeys play their favorite games, swinging from the branches of one-hundred-year-old trees, chattering, scampering on the ground, and often paying social calls on the guests. The monkeys are Asian varieties, but fairly large, and number about three hundred creatures in all. It is certainly a lively scene, and it is quite an experience to be in the midst of so much activity, especially if a monkey decides to sit on your shoulder and go through his instinctive routine of examining your hair for bugs he can pick off and eat. You could spend half a day here and just begin to skim the surface of the social order and family life among the different monkeys.

Nearby, there are attractive picnic grounds where goats, sheep, llamas, donkeys and ducks and other gentle creatures wander around, always ready to accept a handout from your table. For children and adults

Visitors to Thoiry Game Park in France may get a close look at the elephants, or vice versa.

alike, it is a memorable and delightful picnic lunch.

Count Paul recommends a leisurely four- or five-hour auto ride through the rest of the preserve. "It's all right to leave your windows open when you pass the elephant and antelope," Count Paul advises, "but be sure to roll your windows up when you go through lion country. We do not want any accidents!" Feeding lions is not permitted, and special game-park patrol cars are always on the alert to make sure visitors do not stray from the safety of their vehicles.

In the fenced-off area, Thoiry displays fifty-seven lions, the largest group collected anywhere. Count Paul points out that he got seventy baby lion cubs last year —many more than he needs or can keep. He has sent several of them to zoos in North Africa, where ironically lions are now scarce. He hopes it will be possible to do this with other species soon, especially some kinds of antelope which are in short supply in Africa.

The count explains that his lion menagerie comes in at night to the shelter of a lion house, where there are separate quarters for each adult lion. Also there is a room that keeps tons of fresh meat under cold storage, and another that heats the day's food ration to exactly eighty-five degrees before serving.

Watching the lions lazily sunning themselves, or prowling slowly around, or sitting on rocks, gives an observer the impression that they are entirely calm. "Lions are peaceful, actually," says the count. "They would not likely attack us if we were on foot. But there is always some danger—you cannot predict exactly, and besides, it is bad for lions or other wild animals to be around people too much. They do not need to be petted or talked to. It is against their nature."

As we passed into the African game area, over one hundred acres of open land, the count explained that here he can keep several different animals in harmony. "None of them is a predator, and they all eat vegetation. My animals get along better here in the open than do their counterparts in zoos with only two or three to a cage. We have enough room for them to run off their excess energy, or to escape if one turns on another."

To see this mingling of beasts, to see zebra and giraffe strolling peaceably near hartebeests and wildebeests, while nearby an elephant rolls its back in the dirt, is a wonderful experience. Some five hundred animals roam and graze together here, and a white rhino pays no attention at all to a group of fleet gazelle who look as though they are playing follow the leader. The count points out that some antelope do have a tendency to fight—and kill—others, but he has been very successful in preventing this by the use of a special indoor maze which allows animals, in effect, to hide from one another.

After visiting the African grounds, it is quite a surprise to come across the count's new park, reserved entirely for bear, and a few rabbits who were there before. "We have a miniature Yellowstone Park," he says. "Only thirty acres, but perhaps you can see so much more here because everything is open to view." And indeed a mother bear lumbered by the roadside, closely followed by two cubs. They did not even seem to notice our presence, but as we watched them veer off into some woods, mama bear looked back once to be sure the two cubs were still following.

Nearly a million people visited Thoiry last year, and Count Paul says he is building similar parks in Belgium

Thoiry Game Park has a special area reserved for bears.

and Italy now, and two more in France. Soon Europe will have as many as America, and, learning from Thoiry's experience, they will all be open zoos.

Last, the count showed us the rather small, more traditional zoo he maintains, with its cages and variety of creatures. "Some day soon," he says, "I shall destroy this zoo. I want all my animals to be able to live free. It is best for them, best for people too. As soon as we can learn enough, how to let them go wild here, we will. It will be a happy day for me when I pull down all these ugly cages."

590.7

11❖Breeding in Zoos

A ZOO OFFICIAL ONCE COMMENTED THAT one mark of a good zoo is its capacity for encouraging its animals to reproduce. It has long been recognized that captivity limits the ability of many wild animals to mate and bear young. Spending a lifetime behind bars, on view for thousands of visitors, has discouraged more than one species from pursuing normal mating habits. For years, the cheetah, and gorilla, the Galapagos tortoise and the Andean condor, to name a few, defied the most imaginative tactics of zookeepers to induce them to bear young while in captivity. The assumption had always been that there was something different about certain animals in captivity. The possibility that the fault actually lay in poor zoo environment tended to be overlooked.

With extinction threatening more and more species of wildlife, biologists and zoo officials have had to revise their thinking. If the leopard, the cheetah, the rhinoceros and the elephant continue to be relentlessly pushed off the plains of Africa, the tiger in India gunned to

Berwyn Public Library

extinction, the birds of prey in Europe and America contaminated by pesticides, then these animals must be provided with another environment where they can live and reproduce, or else they will disappear forever from the face of the earth. If zoos are to preserve wildlife, they have to learn to breed their own rather than replenish their stock with fresh specimens from the wild.

As a result, an increasing number of zoos around the world have become concerned with propagating those species that are endangered. Relying on the admission fees they charge, and certain subsidies or grants, many zoos have been able to undertake research projects. They are studying the reproductive cycle, such as when the female ovulates and when the animals can be bred; what stimulates mating; the mating rituals of the animals; how to bring about pregnancies; and how to raise the young. In just the last five years, the effect of all this research activity has proved dramatic.

For example, the San Diego Zoo, Lion Country Safari in Florida and Whipsnade Park in England (among many others) have made great strides in tackling the problem of cheetah births. Lion Country Safari made available its collection of twenty-five cheetahs, the largest assembled group of this elusive cat, for study by leading international scientists. Out of this research project came a variety of feeding formulas to enhance the cats' health and fertility, along with a better understanding of the behavior patterns of the cheetah. Whipsnade Park actually succeeded in mating a pair of cheetahs, producing two litters of three cubs each. However, it was the San Diego Zoo which scored the biggest breakthrough in discovering why cheetahs have

One of the Galapagos tortoises at the San Diego Zoo. These turtles may weigh over 100 pounds.

been so difficult to breed in captivity. There it was found that cheetahs usually are caged in the same section of the zoo as their archenemy, the lion. Thus, they became too agitated for procreation. By separating the two types of cats, the zoo experts have discovered that the cheetahs can remain calm enough to breed and bring up their offspring.

The San Diego Zoo authorities also unlocked the secret of the Galapagos tortoises. The huge reptiles needed only enough sand in which to dig the nests they require for mating. The turtles, which weigh over one hundred pounds, generally deposit their eggs in a pit dug about eight inches into the sand. The nest itself is about the size of a football.

A great many herd animals, such as antelope, have run into breeding obstacles when put into cages for two. Yet zoos like San Diego, with its one thousand acres, Phoenix, Lion Country Safari and the Thoiry Game Preserve in France, where hoofed animals can roam in herds, have been able to achieve remarkable progress in reproducing these species. Thoiry in France and Lion Country Safari in Florida boast the largest collections of black buck antelope outside of Africa, where the species has become endangered. Lion Country Safari has begun to make inroads in breeding another threatened species among the antelope group, the addax. The Phoenix Zoo has managed to revive the Arabian oryxes from the ashes of extinction. This species of rare antelope, native to Saudi Arabia, began vanishing because Arabian tribesmen covet their corkscrew horns. Eventually, the Phoenix Zoo hopes to breed oryxes in sufficient numbers to restock Saudi Arabia's herd, if the Arabs agree to stop killing them.

The San Francisco Zoo has started to make headway in the reproduction of gorillas by giving these shy simians private rooms, away from the view of spectators, for their courting period. The Bronx Zoo's "World of Darkness," by providing different species with an environment as close as possible to their native habitat, has encouraged active breeding among several species.

Until approximately 1930, the breeding of captive animals was a problem for virtually every zoo in the world. Chimpanzees, which could barely be kept alive, have been bred freely in many places since 1933. The elephant, regarded by Charles Darwin as the classic example of the mammal that would not reproduce in captivity, has been bred in zoos for over forty years. The first rhinoceros ever to be born in captivity appeared in Chicago's Brookfield Zoo in 1941. These early breedings were primarily a triumph of the science of animal biology. Zoo authorities, mostly through trial and error and observation, were able to surmount many of the early obstacles to reproduction by learning the facts about the animal's mating and gestation period and its metabolism. Evidently the psychological needs of these animals for reproduction were satisfied by the conditions of their zoos.

As scientists began to learn more about the physiology and psychology of zoo animals, as well as about their relationship with man, techniques to encourage breeding among wider varieties of species became more sophisticated. For example, it was learned that in a number of instances, the very presence of a zoo curator or attendant was enough to inhibit animals from breeding, simply because of the animals' instinctive fear and distrust of man. Thus, it was concluded that where

Two Arabian oryxes at the Los Angeles Zoo. The unicorn fable is based upon this rare antelope. LOS ANGELES ZOO

wild creatures have never overcome their desire to flee from man, they should be placed in environments where man's presence is not felt by them.

In other instances, especially in the case of wild birds, breeding is frequently hindered by the fact that a creature actually identifies with a human being, instead of a member of its own species. This is called imprinting, and frequently occurs when the creature has been hand-reared by a human from infancy. In the case of birds, the human companion will be first accepted as parent, later as friend, and eventually as sex object. With owls it has been discovered that a male and female, hand-raised from infancy together, are often unable to mate because of this imprinting.

Getting a male and female animal to adjust sympathetically to one another often depends on finding the proper setting, so that no outside factors get in the way of nature. Putting a herd animal into a cage for two for the purpose of breeding seems simple, but has often proved a dismal failure. In one classic case a zebra stallion showed strong resentment at being confined with one mare, when his instincts propelled him to covet other females. As a result, he refused to have anything to do with the one mare and eventually bit her to death.

Among wild animals, psychological readiness for breeding cannot take place without some sort of special ceremony or ritual. In fish and birds, this ceremony can be amazingly complicated, and is usually incorporated into a time-place pattern. According to William Conway, director of the Bronx Zoo, "A bird that needs a vertical twig for a particular part of its courtship, or a reptile that requires cyclical temperature change, is more likely to reproduce when the proper ecological furniture is provided.

Zookeepers have to learn these special requirements. For wild birds, it has been discovered that cages emphasizing height rather than length tend to encourage reproduction better, although a bird like the Philippine monkey-eating eagle would need a cage as high as the Houston Astrodome to perform its mating dance in the air.

Even uncomplicated relationships between animals, requiring the least amount of ceremony, can be drastically disturbed if the animal can find no place free from disturbance. This holds true whether the disturbance is caused by man or other animals, including even members of the same species, who sometimes can be very inhibiting.

At Lion Country Safari in Florida, about twelve miles outside West Palm Beach, adult lions are relatively free to move about inside a 640-acre area which is enclosed by steel chain fencing and moats. But the area is subdivided into sections to permit the cheetah and other species like zebra, giraffe, impala, wildebeest, eland and ostrich to exist unhampered by the lions.

"We are trying to create an environment that is as much like Africa as we can make it," says Harry Shuster, president and chairman of the board of Lion Country Safari. "For the lion we have created a definite sex ratio which in our view would be best for breeding purposes. We have also done this with the other species. In addition we have made it possible for compatible species like the rhino, the zebra, the giraffe and the gazelle to enjoy social interplay as they do in their natural habitat. The animals could just as well be back

Note the height of this tropical indoor flight cage at the National
Zoological Park in Washington, D. C. THE SMITHSONIAN INSTITUTION

in Africa, drinking at the same waterhole and eating the same food. The only thing that's different is that the predator animals don't have to kill for their food. This environment we think will stimulate the breeding possibilities."

Similar arrangements at the Thoiry Game Park in France achieved spectacular results in lion reproduction. In 1970, fifty adults produced seventy cubs, enough so that the Thoiry officials were able to send a number back to North Africa to help restock the game parks there. Yet, while recent conditions in Africa have not been conducive to the lions' survival, getting them to reproduce in captivity has generally been easy, and because of this the king of the beasts has never really been considered an endangered species.

In a report which they wrote on Lion Country Safari, three biologists, Randall L. Eaton, William York and William Dredge, observed, "The animals are allowed the freedom of movement and social interaction that is a necessary condition not only for healthy-looking specimens but interesting, healthy-acting ones as well. With the obvious exception of predator-prey interactions, the Safari's lions show the full range of behavior seen in wild populations, many of which are rarely observed in animals in the restricted physical and social environment of many traditional zoos."

In past years, more and more zoos throughout the world have been giving top priority to breeding rare and endangered species in their collections. In many cases their efforts have paid off handsomely with the propagation of such animals as the Siberian tiger, snow leopard, brown hyena, American red wolf, maned wolf, pigmy chimpanzee, orangutan, mongoose lemur, golden lion marmoset, mountain gorilla, pigmy hippopotamus, great Indian rhinoceros, onager, black-tailed prairie dog, among others. The question naturally arises of whether the zoos can eventually propagate a sufficient number of endangered species to restock the wilds.

According to Dr. Charles Schroeder of the San Diego Zoo, "The repropagation of species and sending them back into the wilds is a little far off, but it's a possibility. I believe the reason most species have failed to survive in their home area is because they can't cope with the environment there anymore. The California condor is an example. The animal isn't tough enough to get out and stand on its own and consume the carrion and the food that is available. The turkey buzzard and the golden eagle move in and take its food. Since this bird lays only one egg a year and on precarious sites, often kicking the egg off and breaking it, the future looks pretty bleak for the continuation of the California condor as a great, enormous bird of prey." Dr. Schroeder is of the opinion that even getting the California condor to reproduce and survive in captivity is not promising. Some species are apparently doomed despite all efforts by man.

There have been a number of instances where zoos with remarkably strong and healthy male specimens have lent these animals to other zoos for breeding purposes in order to increase the chances of reproducing stronger and healthier offspring. For example, Sabang, a 380-pound red-haired orangutan, acquired quite a reputation for having sired a good percentage of all the orangutans born in America's zoos. In ten years he had made the rounds of some six zoos before settling down at age nineteen at the Miami Monkey Jungle.

In this area of Lion Country Safari various animals live together much as they would in their natural habitat.

The passing back and forth of animal studs between zoos of different cities has become increasingly common in recent years, and it has not been uncommon for zoos of different countries to exchange breeding animals. The results have frequently turned out to be quite satisfactory, although many zoo officials point out that the need to transport a virile male from zoo to zoo for breeding purposes underlines the fact that the species does not have enough suitable males to survive in the wild state.

Many zoo officials and biologists point out that while they have managed to reproduce many endangered species, there are other threatened species they have not been successful with. The problem of breeding koala bears is particularly acute because the Australian government will no longer permit them to be exported. When the San Francisco Zoo found itself with one lone male after the others in the zoo had died, appeals to Australia for a mate were in vain, so San Francisco officials reluctantly shipped off their prize attraction to the San Diego Zoo, which is the only one in the United States with a couple of female koalas. If offspring result, some of the babies will come back to San Francisco.

Another outstanding example of this problem has been the giant panda, that cuddly, black-and-white, bearlike mammal of Tibet. Until recently there were only two males and two females known in captivity outside the zoos of Red China. The London Zoo has a female, the Moscow Zoo a male, and the Pyongyang Zoo in North Korea reportedly has a male and female. Then in 1972, two giant pandas, a male and a female, were turned over to the National Zoo in Washington, D.C. after being given to President Nixon as a gift from the Chinese government. The hope is that as the prospects of lifting the Bamboo Curtain grow brighter, the Chinese will make more of their collection of giant pandas available for propagating the species. Pandas are still quite rare and zoo matings have not yet been successful. It will take several more gift pandas to ensure a stable supply outside China.

Furthermore, the numbers of offspring produced by many of these animals have not been sufficient for restocking the wilds. As a result, the concept of the zoo has been subjected to rethinking and, out of this, more and more experts have begun to stress the importance of greater space for the animals.

A game preserve in South Africa, where the white rhinoceros was considered endangered, has been able to save this species by means of careful conservation and breeding. Under the management of Ian Player, the program to revitalize the white rhino has proved so dramatically successful that the species is no longer considered to be threatened. Last year, South Africa was able to ship some twenty white rhinos to the San Diego Zoo alone, while others were redistributed to various areas in Africa where they had been previously wiped out by natives and hunters. It is doubtful that any success could have been achieved in repropagating the white rhino if its herds had not been permitted to roam familiar-looking stretches of wild plains set aside for it, unhampered by man, disease or lack of food.

According to many observers, the game preserve, compared with other forms of captivity, probably offers animals the best opportunity to reproduce themselves in numbers large enough to eventually restock depleted natural habitats. For restocking purposes, it is generally agreed that animals should be bred in the hundreds. While zoos have come in for a lot of criticism as being too confining and unsuited to the psychological needs of many animals, their stepped-up efforts at breeding endangered species represent a new milestone in wildlife conservation.

Some biologists believe that it is not too far-fetched to envision a future in which game preserves will have replaced the naturally wild areas that have become destroyed by civilization. Located on the outskirts of cities, where land is less expensive, such preserves covering areas of about one thousand acres, will probably take over the functions of zoos, attracting visitors interested in seeing wild animals living in a new balance of nature under man's protection.

Seaquarium (Florida), 62
Shuster, Harry, 88–90, 106, 108
Solomon, King (Biblical), 4

†

Tamiami Trail (Florida), 22
taming process, 34, 36
Thames River, 7
Thoiry Game Park (France), 82, 92–93, 95–96, 98, 102, 108
Tokyo, 62
training, animal, 47
    examples, 47–48, 50
    problems, 50–51, 53

W

Washington, D.C., Zoo, 60, 68, 70, 111
Whipsnade Park Zoo (England), 100

Y

York, William, 108
Yung-lo, Emperor (China), 10

Z

Zoological Gardens of London, 46–47, 51
Zoological Park (Paris), 53

zoos,
    abuses in, 28–29
    in America, 64–71
    animal breeding in, 42–43, 92
    animal escapes from, 36–38
    animal population in, 16, 18
    animal training in, 47
    combining species in, 96
    diet requirements in, 42–43
    early examples of, 3
    and ecological considerations, 76, 78
    economics of, 79–80
    environment within, 1
    examples of good, 60, 62
    during French Revolution, 12
    future of, 72–78, 80–82
    innovations within, 84–89
    location of, 14, 16
    modern history of, 13–19
    oldest, 11–12
    as "prisons," 20–26
    procurement methods of, 27–29
    rare breeds in, 18
    role of, 1
    size of, 16, 18
    space requirements of, 22
    treatment of animals in, 16, 18
Zurich, 38